The Little Book of

Wedding Wit

G000071476

First published in Great Britain in 2011 by Prion

an imprint of the
Carlton Publishing Group
20 Mortimer Street
London W1T 3JW

2 4 6 8 10 9 7 5 3 1

Some of the material in this book was previous

A catalogue record for this book is available from the
British Library

ISBN 978 1 85375 813 3

Printed in China

The Little Book of

Wedding Wit

Over 150 Humorous Quotes on Tying the Knot

Michael Powell

PRION

Introduction

Few occasions generate as much public curiosity and as many conflicting feelings and column inches as a wedding; those of celebrities and commoners alike are always in the news, because a story is always elevated to a drama when it involves a bride and groom.

From the shotgun ceremony
to the absurd excesses of
celebrity nuptials, a wedding
accommodates so many competing
interests that it always treads a path
between high drama and farce.

This is why, time and time again, it
continues to serve up the funnies.

" We've fallen in love
with the wedding industry
when what we need is a
marriage industry. **"**

Bridget Brennan

" Marriage is when you get to keep your girl and don't have to give her back to her parents. **"**

Eric
age six

" There's a way of transferring funds that's even faster than electronic banking. It's called marriage. "

Ronnie Shakes

" To marry is to halve your rights and double your duties. **"**

Arthur Schopenhauer

"It is most unwise for people in love to marry."

George Bernard Shaw

66 Marriage is like a bank account. You put it in, you take it out, you lose interest. **99**

Irwin Corey

> " The appropriate age for marriage is around 18 for girls and 37 for men. "

Aristotle

66 Marriage is a wonderful invention: then again, so is a bicycle repair kit. 99

Billy Connolly

> **"** Marriage isn't a process of prolonging the life of love, but of mummifying the corpse. **"**

P G Wodehouse

" Love is blind – marriage
is the eye-opener. **"**

Pauline Thomason

66 Marriage is bliss.
Ignorance is bliss.
Therefore... **99**

Anon

**“ Marriage isn't a word...
it's a sentence. ”**

King Vidor
The Crawl

❝ Before I met my husband
I'd never fallen in love,
though I've stepped in it
a few times. **❞**

Rita Rudner

"I dunno, she's got gaps,
I got gaps, together
we fill gaps.**"**

Rocky (Sylvester Stallone)
Rocky

66 We married for better or worse – he couldn't do better and I couldn't do worse. **99**

Anon

66 Being married to Marge
is like being married to my
best friend – and he lets me
feel his boobs. **99**

Homer Simpson

❝ I was watching TV and there was a Spice Girls' video on and I said, 'See the girl in the dark short dress? I'm going to marry her'. **❞**

David Beckham

" When *Top Gun* came out my sisters were like, 'Oh, my God, *Top Gun*! Tom Cruise!' And I very confidently said, 'I'm going to marry him one day'… It was just… Why not? He'll like me. I'm fun. "

Katie Holmes

66 I wouldn't be caught dead marrying a woman old enough to be my wife. **99**

Tony Curtis

❝I thought I was promiscuous, but it turns out I was just thorough – to get the right one.**❞**

Russell Brand

" Don't marry the person
you think you can live with;
marry only the individual
you think you can't
live without. **"**

James C Dobson

❝Before you get married you should meet your fiancé's parents. It is not enough that you like his parole officer.**❞**

Phyllis Diller

"A man likes his wife to be just clever enough to appreciate his cleverness, and just stupid enough to admire it."

Israel Zangwill

You've got to be married, haven't you? You can't go through life being happy.

Colin Crompton

"I think men who have a pierced ear are better prepared for marriage. They've experienced pain and bought jewellery.**"**

Rita Rudner

66 Strong women only
marry weak men. **99**

Bette Davis

66 When a man opens a car door for his wife, it's either a new car or a new wife. **99**

Prince Philip, Duke of Edinburgh

66 Men are like a deck of cards. You need a heart to love them, a diamond to marry them, a club to bash his head in with... and a spade to bury him with. 99

Anon

" Every mother generally hopes that her daughter will snag a better husband than she managed to do but she's certain that her boy will never get as great a wife as his father did. "

Anon

"Don't marry someone you would not be friends with if there was no sex between you."

William Glasser

" The first time you marry for love, the second for money, and the third for companionship. **"**

Jackie Kennedy

" Psychiatrists say girls tend to marry men like their fathers. That is probably the reason mothers cry at weddings. "

Anon

❝I like being married for two reasons. One, I got really tired of dating, and two, I got really tired of exercising.**❞**

Jeff Stilson

"If marriage didn't exist, would you invent it? Would you go 'Baby, this shit we got together, it's so good we gotta get the government in on this shit'?**"**

Doug Stanhope

66 Most men, you see, marry
for safety; they choose a
woman who will make them
feel like a man but never
really challenge them
to be one. 99

John Eldredge

Marriage is our last, best chance to grow up.

Joseph Barth

66 A man who marries a woman to educate her falls a victim to the same fallacy as the woman who marries a man to reform him. 99

Elbert Hubbard

❝I think some people are desperate to get married because they want a big white wedding, whereas I get to be the centre of attention every day, so it's not quite so pressing.**❞**

Lucy Porter

"Now, it's true I married my wife for her looks… but not the ones she's been giving me lately.**"**

Jeff Foxworthy

66 Dammit sir, it's your duty to get married. You can't be always living for pleasure. **99**

Oscar Wilde

" I want a man who's kind
and understanding. Is that
too much to ask of
a millionaire? "

Zsa Zsa Gabor

"The way taxes are, you might as well marry for love."

Joe E Lewis

"When you see what some women marry, you realize how they must hate to work for a living."

Helen Rowland

" If a man works like a horse for his money, there are a lot of girls anxious to take him down the bridal path. **"**

Marty Allen

Ray: Please marry me, Bev, because I'm shit without you.

Beverly: Oh, how romantic ...a marriage proposal that contains the word 'shit'.

Riding in Cars with Boys

66 It is always incomprehensible
to a man that a woman
should ever refuse an offer
of marriage. 99

Jane Austen

66 I literally stalked her for weeks until she said yes. They say it's not stalking if she says yes. **99**

Josh Duhamel
on Fergie

66 My most brilliant achievement was my ability to be able to persuade my wife to marry me. **99**

Winston Churchill

66 I'm deluged with marriage proposals. I even get naked photos. Some women see me in the same way mountaineers see Everest – I'm a big challenge but they still want to mount me and stick a flag at the top. **99**

Alan Carr

" Will you marry me? Ayda Field, I love you so much. Do you mind being my betrothed for the end of time? **"**

Robbie Williams
proposes during an Australian radio interview

"A woman might as well propose: her husband will claim she did."

Edgar Watson Howe

" Will you marry me?
Did he leave you any money?
Answer the second
question first. **"**

Groucho Marx

66 Marry me and you'll be farting through silk for the rest of your life. **99**

Robert Mitchum

"A husband is what is left of the lover after the nerve is extracted."

Helen Rowland

"It has been said that a bride's attitude towards her betrothed can be summed up in three words: Aisle, Altar, Hymn."

Frank Muir

" Why does a woman work
10 years to change a man's
habits and then complain that
he's not the man she married? **"**

Barbra Streisand

❝ Weddings are never about the
bride and groom, weddings
are public platforms for
dysfunctional families. **❞**

Lisa Kleypas
Blue-Eyed Devil

"I didn't have a big fat Greek wedding, but I have a lot of fat Greek friends.**"**

Pete Sampras

" I hate weddings. When I go to weddings, they all say, 'You'll be next!' What I do now is, when I go to funerals, I say to the relatives, 'You'll be next!' That shuts them up. **"**

Paul O'Grady

"I never go to weddings. Waste of time. Person can get married a dozen times. Lots of folks do… But a funeral, that's different. You only die once.**"**

Edna Ferber
Giant

**" Just because I have rice
on my clothes doesn't mean
I've been to a wedding.
A Chinese man threw
up on me. "**

Phyllis Diller

" We're trying to work out a date between the World Cup and the end of the Formula 1 season. **"**

Bryan McFadden
makes his priorities clear

**" A bridegroom is a man
who is never important at
a wedding unless he fails
to show up. "**

Anon

" Money can't buy you happiness, so you might as well give your money to us. "

Dave Barry
on the wedding industry

66 June is the traditional month for weddings. The other 11 are for divorce. **99**

Joe Hickman

"Always get married early in the morning. That way, if it doesn't work out, you haven't wasted a whole day.**"**

Mickey Rooney

66 Everyone can relate to the frustrations that a wedding involves, such as arguing about stuff you don't really care about. **99**

Ed Byrne

" We wanted to get married, but I didn't want to put on a big frock and pay for everyone to have a chicken dinner. I didn't want a register office wedding either. Those are like 'Oh, we're married now apparently. What's on the telly?' **"**

Jo Caulfield

"The average British wedding emits more CO_2 than 10 return flights to Thailand."

BBC Bloom

" Don't sweat the small stuff. In the end, the colour of the flowers doesn't matter. **"**

Beth Ostrosky

> **"** Never get married in the morning, because you never know who you'll meet that night. **"**

Paul Hornung

" Planning the wedding is a trial run for your future marriage. **"**

Tina B Tessina

66 We like the evenings – I just don't see the point in getting up early to get married. **99**

Dita Von Teese
(when married to Marilyn Manson)

66 My wife and I were married in a toilet; it was a marriage of convenience. 99

Tommy Cooper

"Eighteen thousand quid, that's how much the average wedding costs… My advice: marry a Buddhist. They always want to get married under a tree: 'No problem, love. Oak or larch? It's your big day'."

Jeff Green

" The day of the wedding I got cold feet. Jim had to do a logical cost-benefit analysis of why getting married would be good. We came out in the black. **"**

Gale Anne Hurd
(m. James Cameron)

66 On the morning of the wedding, she was in a complete panic. She said, 'Something old, something new – I've got nothing borrowed and blue!' I said, 'You've got a mortgage and varicose veins, will that do?' 99

Victoria Wood

❝ I can't explain why a bride buys her wedding dress, whereas a groom rents his tux. **❞**

Lou Holtz

66 The modern bride dresses to kill, and she usually cooks the same way. **99**

Anon

" My wife spent a fortune on a wedding dress. Complete waste of money in my mind. She's worn it once. I've worn it more than she has. "

Mike Gunn

" The mother of the bride has a double whammy to contend with. First, people are going to be checking her out to see how well-preserved and well-dressed she is and second, they want to see what the bride is going to look like in a few years' time. "

Helena Frith Powell

" Why do brides wear white? Because it's the most popular colour for kitchen appliances. "

Anon

" I bought my best hat for my wedding. It was a real good hat – it outlasted my marriage. **"**

Bill McCoin

" I couldn't believe the groom was married in rented shoes. You're making a commitment for a lifetime and your shoes have to be back by 5:30. "

Jerry Seinfeld

"Since Americans throw rice at weddings, do Asians throw hamburgers?"

Steven Wright

66 We ran out of classical music – that's how long this wedding went on. 99

Richard Lewis

"A wedding is a funeral where you smell your own flowers."

Eddie Cantor

66 All weddings are similar,
but every marriage
is different. **99**

John Berger

" Two TV aerials meet on a roof, fall in love, get married. The ceremony was rubbish but the reception was brilliant. **"**

Tommy Cooper

❝I had a fairytale wedding – Grimm.❞

Marti Caine

“ We need to alter the wedding vow. Till death do us part – or until you become an inconvenience. **”**

Carl Young

" In olden times, sacrifices were made at the altar, a practice that still continues. **"**

Helen Rowland

" 'The Wedding March' always reminds me of the music played when soldiers go into battle. **"**

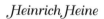

Heinrich Heine

"I always cry at weddings, especially my own."

Humphrey Bogart

" I wish them a long and happy life. If it's as long as their wedding, I'm sure they'll be fine. "

Michael Palin

"A limbo dancer married a locksmith yesterday... the wedding was low-key."

Anon

66 Every time I go to one of my friend's weddings I'm sat on the table with the only other gay man, and we never have anything in common. It's always me who has to praise him for conducting such a beautiful service. 99

Paul Sinha

66 Wedding rings are more than just symbols of eternity. They're magic curses made with backwards-speaking Latin. **99**

Michael Loftus

"Wedding rings: the world's smallest handcuffs."

Homer Simpson

"Marriage requires a person to prepare four types of ring: Engagement Ring, Wedding Ring, Suffering, Enduring."

Anon

" I don't know which was worse, the cost of the bridesmaid dress or having to wear it. **"**

Debbie Etchings

66 If I can't get drunk at a wedding and sleep with a bridesmaid then I don't want to go. **99**

Lloyd Langford

66 I'd like to thank you for your presence and thank you for your presents. **99**

Steve Harris
brief wedding speech

"Our dog died from licking our wedding picture."

Phyllis Diller

" They put these one-time use cameras out on the tables. I thought that was a great idea – 'till they got them pictures back, realized only them little bad kids had the cameras. They're going through hundreds of pictures like, 'Oh, here's another one of the cat's butt'. "

Clinton Jackson

" It was in the size and shape of – how can I put this politely? A pair of boobs. **"**

Emma Thompson
on the wedding cake that was
supposed to evoke the Scottish hills

"The most dangerous food is wedding cake."

James Thurber

" You can always spot the father of the bride – he's the one signing over his retirement fund to the caterer. **"**

Joe Hickman

66 No matter what kind of music you ask them to play, your wedding band will play it in such a way that it sounds like 'New York, New York'. **99**

Dave Barry

❝I love DJs at weddings, DJs that talk all night and you can't understand a word they say.**❞**

Peter Kay

“Don't get divorced or I want my juicer back.”

Jim Jeffries

"I was going to get them a dinner service, but I'm not actually convinced the marriage would last, so I settled for two picnic baskets."

Victoria Wood

❝ I'm all for trial marriages. The wedding of two virgins starts off with a huge handicap. **❞**

Sean Connery

"Getting married for sex is like buying a 747 for the free peanuts."

Jeff Foxworthy

" I was like any new bride, who said, 'I'm going to cook for my man'. In fact, once I started a small kitchen fire in a pan. Smoke was pouring from the pan, and I got really scared. **"**

Catherine Zeta-Jones

66 The wedding and the honeymoon are probably the furthest thing from marriage. **99**

Joseph Simmons

" Next to hot chicken soup, a tattoo of an anchor on your chest, and penicillin, I consider a honeymoon one of the most overrated events in the world. **"**

Erma Bombeck

> " We went to Mexico on our honeymoon, and spent the entire two weeks in bed. I had dysentery. "

Woody Allen

"The honeymoon is over when he phones to say he'll be late for supper and she's already left a note that it's in the refrigerator."

Bill Lawrence

66 What do you have against honeymoons? It is basically sex with room service. **99**

Samantha Jones (Kim Cattrall)
Sex and the City

66 The honeymoon is over when she starts wondering what happened to the man she married, and he starts wondering what happened to the girl he didn't. 99

Anon

"Marriage is like a phone call in the night: first the ring, and then you wake up."

Evelyn Hendrickson

66 I think gay marriage is something that should be between a man and a woman. **99**

Arnold Schwarzenegger

" I'm gay, so why would I want to get married? I'd prefer my sex life to continue. **"**

Scott Capurro

"In Hollywood, brides keep the bouquets and throw away the groom."

Groucho Marx

> **"** I didn't really understand my pre-nup but it was written in Vietnamese by a sobbing father. **"**

Jimmy Carr

> " Ah, yes, 'divorce'. From the Latin for 'having your genitals torn off through your wallet'. "

Robin Williams

66 I can't for the life of me understand why people keep insisting that marriage is doomed. All five of mine worked out. 99

Peter de Vries

" In Britain two out of three marriages end in divorce. The other one ends in murder. **"**

Jeff Green

Marriage is just the first step towards divorce.

Zsa Zsa Gabor

"Love is grand; divorce is a hundred grand.**"**

Anon

> **" I respect a woman too much to marry her. "**

Sylvester Stallone

"A man in love is incomplete until he is married. Then he's finished.**"**

Zsa Zsa Gabor

"I think I'd rather get run over by a train."

Madonna
on getting married again

❝ Any intelligent woman
who reads the marriage
contract, and then goes into
it, deserves all
the consequences. **❞**

Isadora Duncan

" Women now have choices. They can be married, not married, have a job, not have a job, be married with children, unmarried with children. Men have the same choice we've always had: work, or prison. "

Tim Allen

" Instead of getting married again, I'm going to find a woman I don't like and just give her a house. **"**

Rod Stewart

“ I've sometimes thought of marrying, and then I've thought again. **”**

Noël Coward

❝If I ever marry, it will be
on a sudden impulse – as
a man shoots himself. **❞**

HL Mencken

" Sometimes I wonder if men and women really suit each other. Perhaps they should live next door and just visit now and then. **"**

Katharine Hepburn

66 The only good husbands stay bachelors: they're too considerate to get married. 99

Finley Peter Dunne

" I'd marry again if I found a man who had 15 million and would sign over half of it to me before the marriage and guarantee he'd be dead within a year. **"**

Bette Davis

" We're not actually married. We've been together a long time. 'Girlfriend' doesn't seem significant enough a term to describe the relationship; 'lodger' – she hates that. **"**

Sean Lock

❝It would have been a wonderful wedding – had it not been mine.❞

Erma Bombeck

" Any young man who is
unmarried at the age
of 21 is a menace to
the community. **"**

Brigham Young

"My ex-girlfriend called. She's getting married; she called to tell me. Yeah, she called. She wanted closure. I said, 'What part of us not talking the last year seemed open to you?'"

Cash Levy

" I've only slept with men I've been married to. How many women can make that claim? **"**

Elizabeth Taylor

"I'm an excellent housekeeper. Every time I get a divorce, I keep the house."

Zsa Zsa Gabor

I am thinking of taking a fifth wife. Why not? Solomon had a 1,000 wives and he is a synonym for wisdom.

John Barrymore

❝I'm the only man who has a marriage licence made out, 'To Whom It May Concern'.**❞**

Mickey Rooney

"I think that everyone should get married at least once, so you can see what a silly, outdated institution it is.**"**

Twice-divorced
Madonna

66 Marriage is a lot like the Army: everyone complains, but you'd be surprised at the large number that re-enlist. **99**

James Garner

> **"My toughest fight was with my first wife."**

Muhammad Ali

" For her fifth wedding,
the bride wore black and
carried a scotch and soda. **"**

Phyllis Battelle

66 I always say a girl must get married for love – and just keep on getting married until she finds it. **99**

Zsa Zsa Gabor

" I've been married three times – and each time I married the right person. **"**

Margaret Mead

66 I believe in the institution of marriage and I intend to keep trying until I get it right. 99

Richard Pryor

"One of the first things a bridegroom learns is that a man can't fool his wife as easily as his mother.**"**

Anon

❝ If you marry a man who cheats on his wife, you'll be married to a man who cheats on his wife. **❞**

Ann Landers

“My marriage ended on my wedding day.”

Bianca Jagger

" 'What's a couple?'
I asked my mum. She said,
'Two or three'. Which
probably explains why her
marriage collapsed. "

Josie Long

66 When a girl marries she exchanges the attentions of many men for the inattention of one. **99**

Helen Rowland

" Men look at women the way men look at cars. Everyone looks at Ferraris. Now and then we like a pickup truck, and we all buy station wagons. **"**

Tim Allen

**"Marriage is forever.
It's like cement."**

Peter O'Toole

❝ I promise to love, honour and cherish you – for about two days a month. **❞**

Bill Dwyer
on polygamist wedding vows

66 Marriage is based on the theory that when a man discovers a particular brand of beer exactly to his taste, he should at once throw in his job and go to work in the brewery. **99**

George Nathan

66 If the grass looks greener
on the other side of the fence,
it's because they take better
care of it. **99**

Cecil Selig

"Oh, I don't mind going to weddings, just as long as it's not my own."

Tom Waits

" If you're going to do something like getting married, it should have a sense of celebration to it. It should be grand – it doesn't have to be in tracksuits. **"**

Marilyn Manson

66 Never get married in college; it's hard to get a start if a prospective employer finds you've already made one mistake. **99**

Elbert Hubbard